FASHION FOR
WEDDINGS

FASHION FOR
WEDDINGS

images
Publishing

First published in Australia in 1997 by
The Images Publishing Group Pty Ltd
ACN 059 734 431
6 Bastow Place, Mulgrave, Victoria 3170
Australia
Tel: +(61 3) 9561 5544   392.54 FAS
Fax: +(61 3) 9561 4860
e-mail: books@images.com.au

Fashion for Weddings

ISBN: 1 875 498 63 X

Printed in Hong Kong

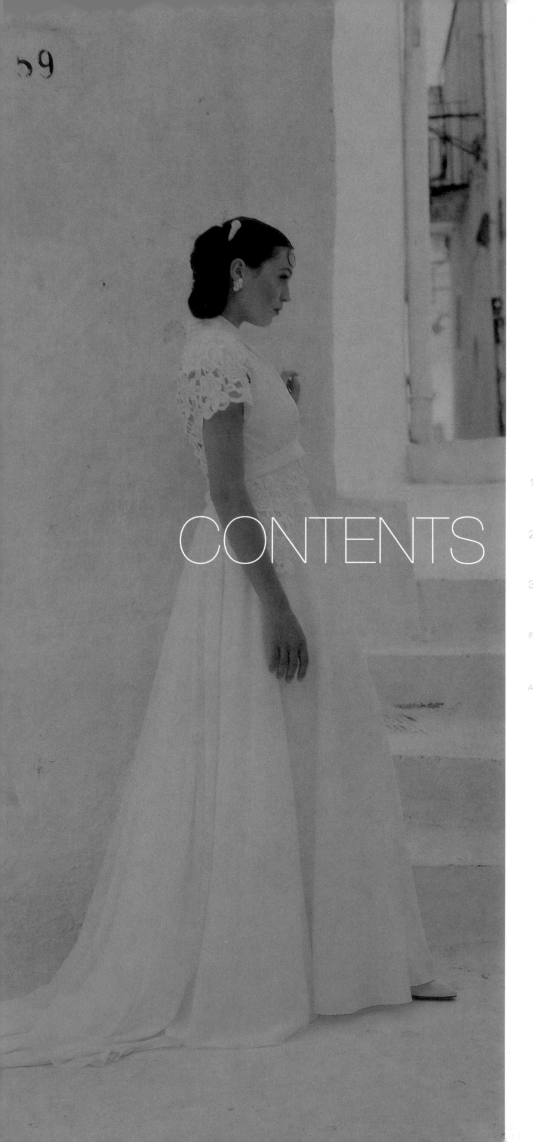

CONTENTS

WEDDING DRESSES

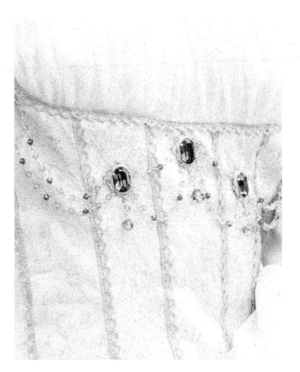

Opposite Page: *Afective Formal and Bridal Wear:* Ivory Thai silk gown with interesting placement of gold piping down bodice seams and at waistline further accentuating the flattering, fitted, long-line bodice. Full skirt with box pleats ends with a traditional train

Above Left: Detail of panelled bodice

Above Right: This feminine olde worlde 2 piece gown features ivory, blush pink and gold brocade panelled bodice with shirred georgette upper bodice, complemented with soft flowing georgette skirt

Photo credit: Rob Stambulic

Above:
Afective Formal and Bridal Wear: Antique gold late medieval inspired gown
features fitted torso that clings to the body as far as the hips. Decorative
gold and bronze braid and delicate jewellery provide the perfect finish

Opposite Page:
Off-the-shoulder silk sheath features silk satin rosettes along neckline and
at opening at centre front hem. Sheath is completed with short brush train
and matching roses

Photo credit: Rob Stambulic

Top:
Afective Formal and Bridal Wear:
Extravagant de lustred satin gown features a fitted bodice, long slender sleeves, a slimline sheath with full and long overskirt richly adorned with gold cornelli trim

Above:
Detail of gold cornelli trim

Opposite Page:
Pre-Raphaelite inspired gown features delicate shirring at upper bodice with the use of opulent silver embroidery on tight fitting bodice for a dramatic contrast. The full skirt reveals deep box pleats from the waist

Photo credit: Rob Stambulic

Opposite Page:
Angelina Baccini: Silk satin has been hand-painted and embroidered in gold chain stich and cornelli in this princess-line style

Top:
Cotton velvet has been used in this fully-boned bodice, cream organza layers flow in the full-gathered skirt and silk georgette draped over the top of the arm. Ribbon embroidery frames a portrait of a lady

Above:
Detail of ribbon embroidery

Photo credit: Jaquie Henshaw

Above Left: *Angelina Baccini:* Detail of pleated, structured skirt

Above Right: Pale pink de lustred satin flows in this knife-pleated skirt complemented by a pearled bodice and features sunray pleated organza cuffs

Opposite Page: Hand-knitted lace has been used to give a body-suit effect over this pleated, structured skirt

Photo credit: Jaquie Henshaw

Opposite Page: *Angelina Baccini*: Ivory de lustred satin is the base for this straight gown with detachable train laced up at the back and embroidered in gold

Above Left: English pure silk damask 50s style gown featuring pleated shawl-collar, hand-made roses and Dior half-bow

Above Right: Detail of hand-made roses and Dior half-bow

Photo credit: Jaquie Henshaw

Opposite Page: *Angelina Baccini:* Straight skirt is hidden under this rich box pleated gown featuring an off-the-shoulder neckline. Hand-beading accentuates the waistline

Above Left: Detail of hand-crocheted tassels

Above Right: Hand-knitted fabric has been used in this short jacket; the tassels and trims have been hand-crocheted, complementing a strapless, box pleated gown

Photo credit: Jaquie Henshaw

Opposite Page:

Romeo Bastone Bridal Couture:
Bodice of silk organza with French lace and hand-petalled rose.
Bouffant skirt is made of silk taffeta and underskirt of shot taffeta

Photo credit: Astir Studio

Top:
Detail of chantilly-lace

Above:
Thai silk gown features bodice and sleeves of chantilly
lace highlighted by gold beading

Photo credit: J. Roubos Video & Photography

Above and Opposite Page:

Romeo Bastone Bridal Couture: Thai silk sheath with coloured French lace applique on bodice and sleeves.
Detachable train features coloured French lace, CB organza bow, and tails

Photo credit: Bonney Leder Photography

Above:

Romeo Bastone Bridal Couture: Thai silk gown of guipure lace appliqued over bodice and sleeves; skirt is bouffant in shape with guipure lace featured on hemline

Photo credit: courtesy of Romeo Bastone Bridal Couture

Opposite Page:

Elegant gown features an off-the-shoulder bodice of metallic French calais lace, silk georgette ruching across the midriff, and a full Thai silk skirt extending into a train

Photo credit: The Studio Photographers

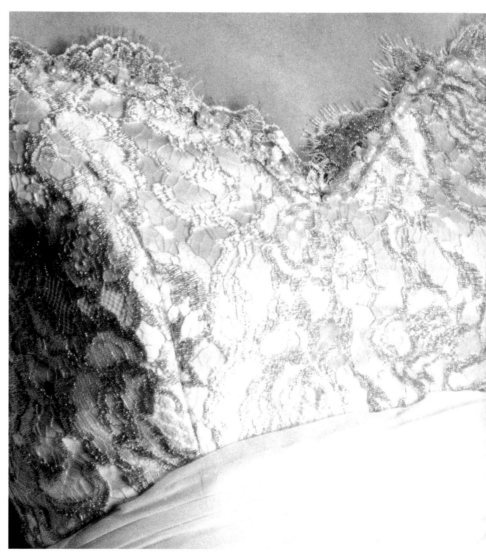

Left:

Romeo Bastone Bridal Couture: French calais lace bodice and sleeves, midriff in ruched chiffon; sleeves form elongated bell shape with matching chiffon skirt

Right:

Detail of lace bodice

Photo credit: Christina Kingston Photography

Above: De lustred satin gown; bodice consists of guipure lace and sleeves with hand-made rosettes. Back features peplum with rosette detailing

Photo credit: Jann Dunn Photography & Associates

Opposite Page & Top:
Romeo Bastone Bridal Couture:
Ivory German velvet bodice with A-line skirt of ivory
duchess silk satin; bodice features beaded French
lace with matching baby pink tulle train

Above:
Detail of bodice featuring beaded French lace

Photo credit: J. Roubos Video & Photography

Left, Right & Opposite Page: Gowns by *Michelangelo Bellantuono*: San Severo, Italy

Photo credit: courtesy of Michelangelo Bellantuono

Above & Opposite Page:
Gowns by *Michelangelo Bellantuono:* San Severo, Italy

Photo credit: courtesy of Michelangelo Bellantuono

Opposite Page: *Betrothed Bridal Boutique:* Traditional silk dresses

Photo credit: Stills Photography

Above Left: Part of the Betrothed Australiana Collection; features halter neck style covered in opal coloured flowers

Photo credit: The Advertiser paper

Above Right: Hand-embroidered bodice features lattice trim front and subtle shoulder roses, hem is hand-painted with roses

Photo credit: John Venus Photography

Above:
Betrothed Bridal Boutique: Medieval inspired gown of pure silk brocade and satin trim

Opposite Page:
Pure silk gown features hand-smocking on bodice and hand-painted hem detail

Photo credit: Oz Photography

Opposite Page & Top:
Bridal Boutique:
Off-the-shoulder dress in princess satin
with beaded bodice and beading
featured on front of the full skirt

Above:
Detail of beading

Photo credit: Greg Semu

Above & Opposite Page:

Bridal Boutique: Sweetheart neckline with guipure lace bodice in Thai silk featuring small hand-made roses with pearl beading on the train

Photo credit: Greg Semu

Above Left: | *Bridal Boutique:* Detail of hooped skirt

Above Right: | Straight dress featuring a shawl collar, beaded front, and detachable train highlighted with deep lace insets and burgundy roses; for the fuller figure

Opposite Page: | For the bride with a fuller figure, off-the-shoulder gown in princess satin featuring hand-made red and white roses and hooped skirt

Photo credit: Greg Semu

Top & Above:
Carmi Couture Collection: Detail of yoke and
chantilly lace

Opposite Page:
Sophisticated chantilly lace sheath, pointed espirit
yoke and chiffon detachable train

Photo credit: Buckmaster Photography

Above:

Carmi Couture Collection: Detail of guipure lace and rose design

Opposite Page:

Glamorous ivory duchess satin sheath, sleeveless guipure lace
bodice in a lattice and rose design

Photo credit: Buckmaster Photography

52

Opposite Page:
Carmi Couture Collection: Guipure lace bodice,
draped silk skirt with bustle-back and silk flowers

Top:
Cathedral split chiffon veil complements this guipure
lace and silk shantung gown

Above:
Detail of bodice

Photo credit: Buckmaster Photography

Above Left: *Carmi Couture Collection:* Detail of multi-tiered skirt

Above Centre: Guipure lace bodice with multi-tiered silk gazaar skirt

Above Right: Detail of double-tiered border

Opposite Page: Hand-beaded French alencon lace sheath, double-tiered border and detachable chiffon train

Photo credit: Buckmaster Photography

Above & Opposite Page:
Gown by *The Cotswold Frock Work Shop*

Photo credit: courtesy of The Cotswold Frock Work Shop

Left & Right: | Gowns by *The Cotswold Frock Work Shop*

Photo credit: courtesy of The Cotswold Frock Work Shop

Above:

Gown by *The Cotswold Frock Work Shop*

Photo credit: courtesy of The Cotswold Frock Work Shop

Above:
Elina Bridal by Jane Yeh: Ivory empire-line gown with embroidered dupion silk bodice and georgette cross-cut skirt

Photo credit: Lesley Walker

Opposite Page:
Classical gold embroidered and beaded dupion silk gown

Photo credit: Polly Walker

Above Left: *Richard Glasgow, Inc.*: Detail of sleeves

Above Right: Hand-made silk flowers trim sleeves of silk-faced satin gown

Opposite Page: Hand-made silk flowers frame neckline of fitted torso bodice which complements a fully gathered tulle skirt

Photo credit: Elliot Siegel

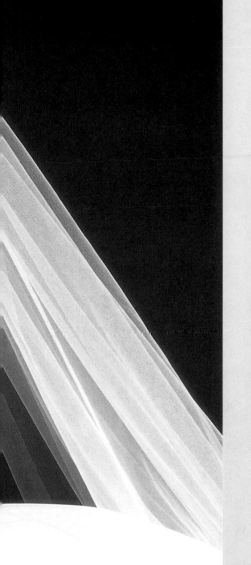

Opposite Page: *Richard Glasgow, Inc.:* Fitted guipure lace bodice has battaell neckline and floor length silk satin organdy skirt

Above Left: Detail of beaded French lace on bodice

Above Right: Beaded French alencon lace trims bodice of scoop neck off-the-shoulder A-line gown of silk-faced satin

Photo credit: Elliot Siegel

Top:
Richard Glasgow, Inc.: Hand-made silk flowers surround
neckline and cascade down front of 3ply silk shantung
princess-line gown

Opposite Page:
Multi-sized pearls trim silk-faced gown with full skirt and chapel length train

Photo credit: Elliot Siegel

Top:

House of Elegance: Detail of gold pattern on train

Opposite Page:

Gold pattern ivory dupion silk gown, gold piping and gold cornelli

Photo credit: Alex Bult Photography

Above Left: Inatome International: Detail of lace pattern

Above Centre: V-neck lace sheath with detachable train

Above Right: Detail of beading

Opposite Page: Heavily beaded empire with slim sheath gown

Photo credit: courtesy of Inatome International

PETER
LANGNER

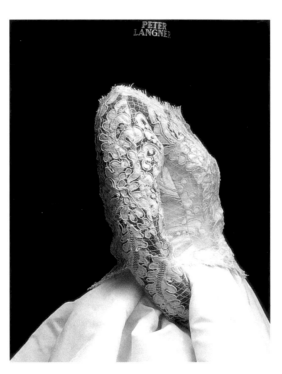

Opposite Page: | *Peter Langner:* Fitted Regency jacket with train covers a simple satin sheath

Above Left: Grand simplicity is created with a cascading train

Above Centre: Jacket of re-embroidered lace tops a voluminous skirt with back fullness

Above Right: Fitted Mikado silk jacket worn over layers of tulle

Photo credit: Arturo Patten

Above:
Peter Langner: Gown of silk Mikado with distinctive beading

Opposite Page:
Cotton macrame is woven with ribbons and chord to create a bell-skirted gown

Photo credit: Amadeo Volpe

Above Left:	*Shane McConnell Couture:* French lace bodice with Thai silk skirt in pale pink with silk organza overlay
Above Centre:	Detail of French ribbon lace
Above Right:	French ribbon lace bodice with tulle full-circle skirt
Opposite Page:	Duchess satin strapless gown with red printed tulle skirt and strapless gown with gold embroidered bodice and skirt featuring all-in-one shawl

Photo credit: Brett Ockleshaw, Image Solutions

Above Left:	*Shane McConnell Couture:* Lemon-coloured guipure lace bodice with a Thai white silk pleated midriff skirt
Above Centre:	French chantilly lace with silk duchess satin skirt and bow
Above Right:	Silk strapless duchess satin ivory gown with beaded bodice
Opposite Page:	Guipure lace and silk organza skirt with silk parcel bow

Photo credit: Brett Ockleshaw, Image Solutions

Left: Silk gold embroidered upper bodice with a full-circle silk organza skirt

Right: Detail of bodice

Photo credit: Brett Ockleshaw, Image Solutions

Top:
Shane McConnell Couture: Ivory duchess satin gown with glass beaded neckline

Opposite Page:
Ice-blue pure silk strapless fully beaded bodice gown with full trailing bustle

Photo credit: Brett Ockleshaw, Image Solutions

Above:

Shane McConnell Couture:
Embroidered silk organza strapless gown with sew-in-one bustle tails

Opposite Page:

French navy blue chantilly lace bodice with pure silk duchess skirt and bow

Photo credit: Brett Ockleshaw, Image Solutions

Opposite Page: | *The Marisa Collection:* Tamara Kristen for The Marisa Collection

Above Left: | Detail

Above Right: | Tamara Kristen for The Marisa Collection

Photo credit: Brides Magazine

Opposite Page: Gown by *Rapsimo*

Above Left: Detail

Above Right: Gown by *Rapsimo*

Photo credit: Belinda Mason

Above & Opposite Page:
Gowns by *Rapsimo*

Photo credit: *Oz Photography*

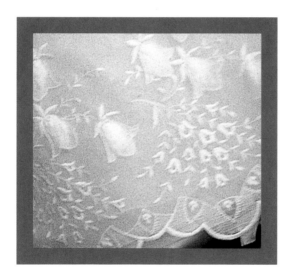

Opposite Page & Top:
Gowns by *Rapsimo*

Above:
Detail

Photo credit: Oz Photography

Opposite Page & Above Right: Gowns by *Rapsimo*

Above Left: Detail

Photo credit: Oz Photography

Above & Opposite Page:
Gowns by *Rapsimo*

Photo credit: Belinda Mason

Above & Opposite Page:
Gowns by *Rapsimo*

Photo credit: Oz Photography

Top & Above:
Detail of beading

Opposite Page:
Gown by *Rapsimo*

Photo credit: Oz Photography

Above:
Detail of back

Opposite Page:
Gown by *Rapsimo*

Photo credit: Oz Photography

110

Opposite Page & Top:
Gowns by *Rapsimo*

Above:
Detail of bodice

Photo credit: Oz Photography

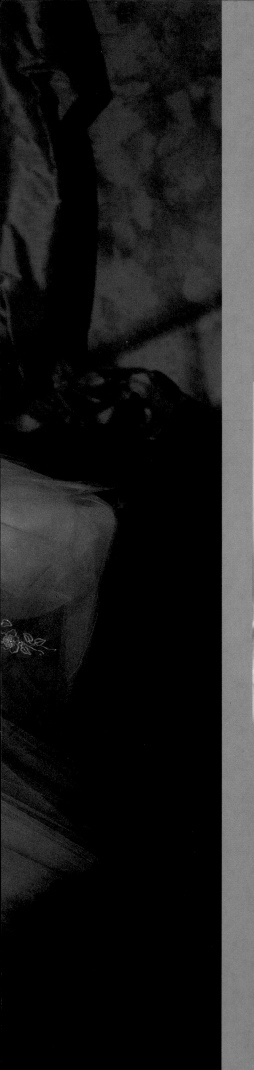

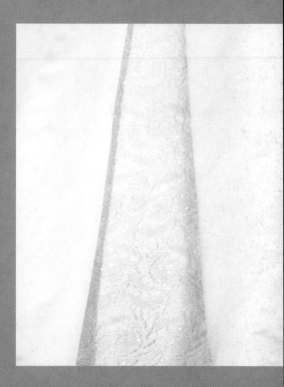

Above Left: *Riccio:* Detail of guipure lace beaded neckline

Above Centre: Beaded guipure lace bodice accents neckline of silk shantung gown with chapel length train

Above Right: Detail of guipure lace appliques

Opposite Page: Beaded guipure lace appliques asymmetrically trim silk shantung off-the-shoulder bodice and fully gathered tulle skirt

Photo credit: Elliot Siegel

Above Left:

Riccio: Floor length tulle skirt highlighted with silk flowers and flower details complements a fitted silk satin bodice

Photo credit: Dyana van Campen

Above Right:

Detail of guipure lace accented with pearls

Opposite Page:

Guipure lace off-the-shoulder bodice accented with pearls, complements fully gathered tulle skirt

Photo credit: Elliot Siegel

Left: *Riccio:* Detail of guipure lace hemline

Right: Guipure lace trims bodice and hemline of off-the-shoulder silk shantung gown with chapel length train

Left: Detail of guipure lace hemline

Right: Guipure lace trims bodice and hemline of off-the-shoulder silk shantung gown with chapel length train

Photo credit: Elliot Siegel

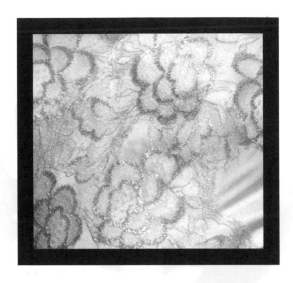

Top & Above:
Connie Simonetti Bridal Couture: Detail of chantilly lace bodice and waistline

Opposite Page:
Pure silk gown with waistline draping; ivory and gold chantilly lace through bodice and sleeves with full skirt

Photo credit: Peter Suveges

Above:
Special Days Bridalwear: Plum velvet bodice with ivory skirt

Opposite Page:
Off-the-shoulder pink satin with beaded bodice and rose trims

Photo credit: Dennis Mann

Above:

Special Days Bridalwear: Black shantung gown with full train and burgundy roses

Photo credit: Dennis Mann

Left: | Full gown with cathedral train in white satin

Right: | Straight ivory crepe with gold silk drape

Photo credit: Dennis Mann

Left:	*Special Days Bridalwear:* Silk empire-line gown with duchess satin bodice
Centre:	Pink satin overlaid in pink tulle
Right:	Long sleeved straight lace dress with gold silk wrap bodice

Above: Straight lace gown with rose trim and detachable tulle train

Photo credit: Dennis Mann

Left & Centre: *Special Days Bridalwear:* Straight strappy silk crepe dress with lace jacket

Right: Straight silk with bodice overlay of Swiss lace

Left:	Empire-line shantung with beaded finish
Centre:	Detail of bead work
Right:	Ivory gown with cathedral train and bead work finish
	Photo credit: Dennis Mann

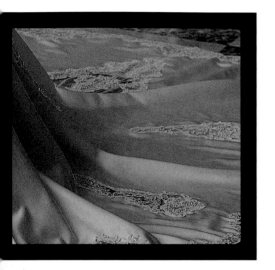  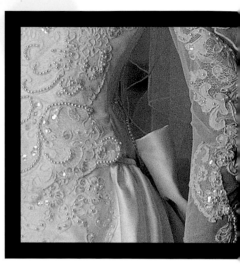

Above Left: *Moonlight Design:* Detail of detachable train

Above Centre: Regal satin sheath with detachable train

Above Right: Detail of satin sheath

Opposite Page: Regal satin jewel-neck gown with alencon lace

Photo credit: Dennis Kugler

Opposite Page:
Italian satin and alencon lace off-the-shoulder gown with monarch length train, beaded in pearls

Photo credit: Dennis Kugler

Above:
Moonlight Design: Pure silk shantung gown with detachable train and illusion lycra bodice

Opposite Page:
Pure silk shantung off-the-shoulder gown with cathedral train

Photo credit: Dennis Kugler

Above Left: *Moonlight Design:* Regal satin gown with alencon lace

Above Centre: Detail of bodice

Above Right: Pure silk shantung gown

Opposite Page: Pure silk shantung gown with beaded Venice lace

Photo credit: Dennis Kugler

Left: *Moonlight Design:* Pure silk shantung sheath gown with detachable train

Right: Pure silk shantung gown with pink petals and monarch train

Photo credit: Dennis Kugler

Above: | Italian satin and organza gown with alencon lace

Photo credit: Dennis Kugler

Above Left: Moonlight Design: Venice lace and tulle gown with detachable cathedral train

Above Centre: Detail of Venice lace bodice

Above Right: Pure silk shantung gown with pink rosettes

Opposite Page: Pure silk shantung gown with beaded bodice

Photo credit: Dennis Kugler

Left: *Moonlight Design:* Regal satin gown with detachable train

Right: Detail of train

Left: | Pure silk shantung sheath gown with Venice lace and detachable train

Right: | Detail of bodice

Photo credit: Dennis Kugler

Opposite Page & Above Right: Gowns by *Sposa Bella Mfg. Ltd.*

Above Left: Detail

Photo credit: Adrian Charles Photography

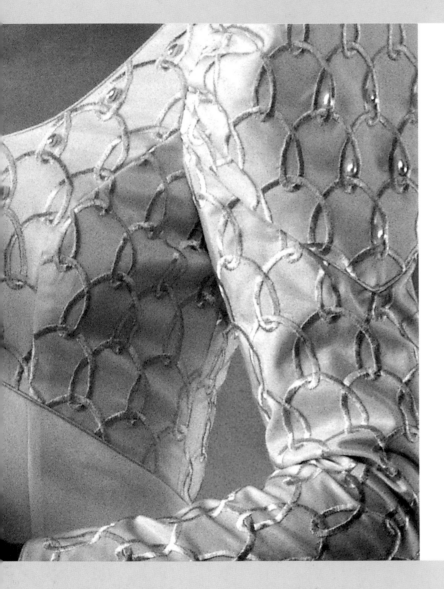

Above Left:	Detail of bodice
Above Right:	Drawing: Empire-line gown with embroidered organza bodice and French satin skirt
Opposite Page:	Gown by *Sposa Bella Mfg. Ltd.*

Photo credit: Adrian Charles Photography

Above & Opposite Page:
Gowns by *Sposa Bella Mfg. Ltd.*

Photo credit: Adrian Charles Photography

Above:

Sposa Bella Mfg. Ltd.: (*Drawing*) Duchess satin gown has embroidered and hand-beaded neckline, hemline and train, fitted front and fullness at back

Opposite Page:

Gown by *Sposa Bella Mfg. Ltd.*

Photo credit: Adrian Charles Photography

Opposite Page:
Gown by *Sposa Bella Mfg. Ltd.*

Top & Above:
Details of bow and bodice

Photo credit: Adrian Charles Photography

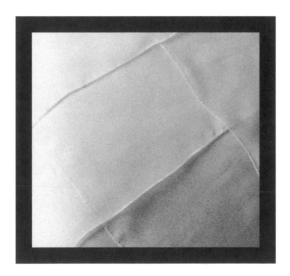

Opposite Page:
Gown by *Sposa Bella Mfg. Ltd.*

Top & Above:
Details of gown

Photo credit: Adrian Charles Photography

Above:

Ellen Walker: Detail of cornelli pattern

Opposite Page:

Long A-line coat in de lustred satin, heavily embellished with cornelli detail, sprinkled with pearl beading, worn over matching sheath dress

Photo credit: Peter Russell

Opposite Page: *Ellen Walker:* Sensuous low back, silk faille gown with flowing fishtail train embellished with cornelli detail

Above Left: Detail of low back

Above Right: Close-up of cornelli detail

Photo credit: Peter Russell

Above: *Young Ming Fashion Bridal Dress Co Ltd*: Details of midriff, neckline and bodice

Opposite Page: Gown by *Young Ming Fashion Bridal Dress Co Ltd*

Photo credit: Hsutsai commercial photo design

HEADWEAR & ACCESSORIES

Above Left:

Afective Formal and Bridal Wear: Straw hat trimmed with ivory and green silk flowers and finished with bridal netting

Photo credit: Rob Stambulic

Above Right & Opposite Page:

Hats by *Christine James Exclusive Classic and Sculptured Millinery*

Photo credit: courtesy of Romeo Bastone

Above Left: *Ines Colosimo Exclusive Millinery and Accessories:* Detail of apricot capura lace

Above Right: Tilted wide brim hat in navy duchess silk fabric trimmed with apricot capura lace, gold handled oval bag trimmed with lace and fabric-covered shoes

Opposite Page: Organza and suede-look fabric top hat with feathers, bag with gold handle and fabric-covered shoes

Photo credit: Ardmillan Studios

Above Left:	Ines Colosimo Exclusive Millinery and Accessories: Silk organza bowed-like shaped hat with diamanté trims
Above Centre:	Detail of chapeau hat
Above Right:	Shot gold and black metallic thread organza, ruche wide-brimmed chapeau hat
Opposite Page:	Black and white big brimmed hat in silk knitted yarn; gondilar swilled shaped bag in silk knitted yarn

Photo credit: Ardmillan Photo Studios

188

Above Left & Opposite Page:

Above Right:

Headwear by *Julie Fleming Model Millinery*

Detail of coronet

Photo credit: courtesy Julie Fleming

Opposite Page:
Headwear by *Rapsimo*

Top & Above:
Hats by *Christine James
Exclusive Classic and
Sculptured Millinery*

Photo credit: Kristina Kingston

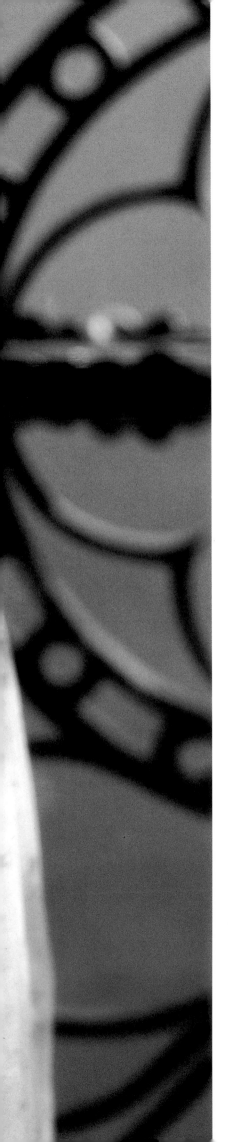

Opposite Page: *Stephanies Bridal Millinery:* This piece created for the New York Bridal Show was the finale in the fashion show receiving a standing ovation, a star-shaped wand also accompanies this headpiece and veil

Above Left: Pure French feminine inspiration, pure elegance for the more adventurous bride; face veil or snood, Swaroski crystal net, diamond antique brooch at side

Above Right: Headpiece designed for the catwalk at the New York Bridal Apparel show is breathtaking in detail, design and finish

Photo credit: Mauro Pomponio

JEWELLERY

Left:

Diamor International Jewellers:
designer and jeweller; Vladimir Tsyskin: Hand-made wedding and engagement rings

Right:

Detail

Photo credit: Brent Ockleshaw, Image Solutions

Above:

Le Diademe: Exclusive range of bridal headpieces and matching earrings

Photo credit: The Portrait Designer

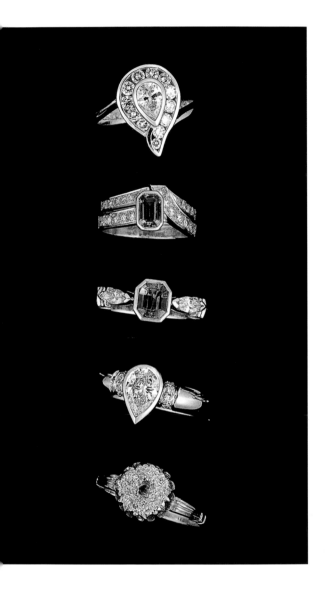

P.B. McMaster & Son: 18ct yellow gold pear-shaped diamond cluster ring with channel set diamonds, 18ct yellow gold emerald cut golden sapphire and diamond engagement ring with diamond set fitted wedder, 18ct yellow gold ceylon sapphire ring with marquise cut diamonds set each side, 18ct yellow gold pear-shaped diamond set ring with diamond set shoulders, 18ct rose gold golden sapphire and diamond traditional cluster ring

18ct yellow gold ring set with one pear-shaped diamond with grain and channel set diamond shoulders, 18ct yellow gold ring set with one natural emerald with marquise shaped diamonds and diamond set shank, 18ct yellow gold engagement ring set with brilliant cut diamond and grain set diamond shoulder with matching grain set wedder, 18ct yellow gold 'modern cluster' ring set with oval, marquise, and brilliant cut diamonds

18ct yellow gold 'Victoria' amethyst and cultured pearl necklet

18ct yellow gold 'bow' style solitaire diamond ring, 18ct yellow gold 'fan' style solitaire diamond ring, 18ct rose, yellow and white gold 'twist' style gents' wedder, 18ct yellow gold diamond set ring with swirl style shoulders and diamonds channel set, 18ct yellow gold pear-shaped diamond set ring with one pear-shaped diamond set either side, 18ct yellow gold pear-shaped diamond cluster ring with channel set diamonds, 18ct yellow gold ceylon sapphire and diamond modern style cluster

Photo credit: courtesy P.B. McMaster & Son

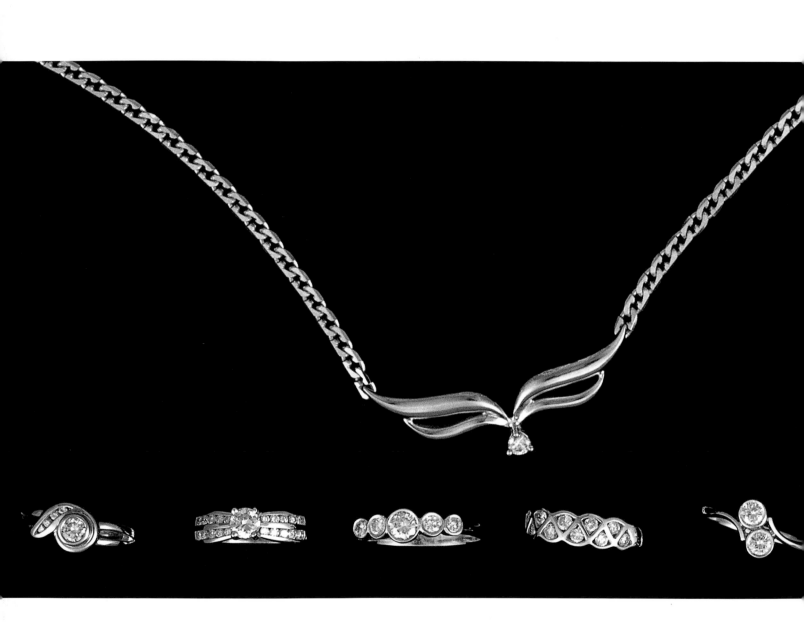

Above: *P.B. McMaster & Son:* 18ct yellow gold diamond set necklet

Below:
(left to right)   18ct yellow gold diamond set ring with swirl style shank and channel set shoulders, 18ct yellow gold diamond set ring with centre diamond in claws and shoulder channel set, 18ct yellow gold five diamond engagement ring, 18ct yellow gold 'basket' style diamond set ring, 18ct yellow gold two brilliant cut diamond ring

Photo credit: courtesy P.B. McMaster & Son

Above: *Jeanette Maree:* A rich blend of the exotic; ruby coloured crystals set into antique gold finish with sprinkle of diamanté to highlight. Tendrils cascade forward over tiara flaunting small crystal droplets, accentuating this unique design

Photo credit: courtesy Jeanette Maree

Left – Right: Necklace, mask and earrings continue theme to complete medieval wedding

Photo credit: courtesy Jeanette Maree

Left: | *Afective Formal and Bridal Wear:* Hand-made crystal tiara worn with complementing gold and crystal strand necklace with centre drop

Photo credit: Rob Stambulic

Right: | *Jeanette Maree:* Two separate necklaces are brought together as a marriage of pearl, crystal beads and matt gold finish chain

Above: Necklet of pearls set into antique gold highlighted with a sprinkle of diamanté

Photo credit: courtesy Jeanette Maree

Above &
Opposite Page:

Jeanette Maree: True to the flower, this simplistic design uses a vivid vine like wire to exhibit the bloom; scattered pearls flow throughout the design as unopened buds do the flower

Photo credit: courtesy Jeanette Maree

INDEX

ACKNOWLEDGMENTS

We wish to thank all participating firms for their valuable contribution
to this publication and especially the following firms who provided
photographs for the following pages:

Pages 4,5:
Inatome International
Photo credit: courtesy of Inatome International

Page 6:
Rapsimo
Photo credit: Belinda Mason

Page 7:
Michelangelo Bellantuono
Photo credit: courtesy of Michelangelo Bellantuono

Page 8, Wedding Dresses Divider:
Betrothed Bridal Boutique
Photo credit: Oz Photography

Page 9, Wedding Dresses Divider:
Peter Langner
Photo credit: Arturo Patten

Page 180, Headwear & Accessories Divider:
Christine James Exclusive Classic and Sculptured Millinery
Photo credit: courtesy of Romeo Bastone

Page 181, Headwear & Accessories Divider:
Julie Fleming Model Millinery
Photo credit: courtesy of Julie Fleming Model Millinery

Pages 198,199, Jewellery Divider:
Jeanette Maree
Photo credit: courtesy of Jeanette Maree

Page 214, Index:
Inatome International
Photo credit: courtesy of Inatome International

Page 215, Index:
Carmi Couture Collection
Photo credit: Buckmaster photography